Ruckus

Jenna Fincke

methuen | drama

LONDON • NEW YORK • OXFORD • NEW DELHI • SYDNEY

METHUEN DRAMA
Bloomsbury Publishing Plc
50 Bedford Square, London, WC1B 3DP, UK
1385 Broadway, New York, NY 10018, USA
29 Earlsfort Terrace, Dublin 2, Ireland

BLOOMSBURY, METHUEN DRAMA and the Methuen
Drama logo are trademarks of Bloomsbury Publishing Plc

First published in Great Britain 2022

Cover graphics by Luke W Robson

Cover photo by The Other Richard

A catalogue record for this book is available from the British Library.

A catalog record for this book is available from the Library of Congress.

ISBN: PB: 978-1-3503-8017-2
ePDF: 978-1-3503-8019-6
eBook: 978-1-3503-8018-9

Series: Modern Plays

Typeset by Mark Heslington Ltd, Scarborough, North Yorkshire

To find out more about our authors and books visit
www.bloomsbury.com and sign up for our newsletters.

Ruckus

by Jenna Fincken

Ruckus was first performed from 3–28 August 2022 at the Cairns Lecture Theatre, Summerhall, at the Edinburgh Fringe Festival 2022. The creative team for this production was as follows:

Performer and Writer	**Jenna Fincken**
Director	Georgia Green
Producer	Joey Dawson for Wildcard
Associate Producer	Rachel Thomas
Sound Designer	Tingying Dong
Movement Director	Christina Fulcher
Lighting and Projection Designer	Simeon Miller
Set and Costume Designer	Jida Akil
Production Manager	Charlotte Ranson
Stage Managers	Lois Sime
	Naomi Shanson

The production subsequently ran from 5–29 October 2022 at the Southwark Playhouse, London. The creative team for this production was as follows:

Performer and Writer	**Jenna Fincken**
Director	Georgia Green
Producer	Joey Dawson for Wildcard
Associate Producer	Rachel Thomas
Sound Designer	Tingying Dong
Movement Director	Christina Fulcher
Lighting and Projection Designer	Simeon Miller
Video Designer	Reuben Cohen
Production Manager	Charlotte Ranson
Stage Manager	Becky Thornton

Jenna Fincken (Performer and Writer)

Jenna is an actress and writer who trained at the Oxford School of Drama. Her most recent success was *Ruckus*, her debut play. This received critical acclaim at the Edinburgh Fringe Festival 2022, garnering numerous four- and five-star reviews. Jenna was the First Finalist for the Popcorn New Writing Award, nominated for the Filipa Bragança Award and received a Lustrum Award for her 'unforgettable' performance and new writing. Professional acting credits include *Ruckus* (Summerhall, Edinburgh Fringe), *People, Places and Things* (Headlong, Oxford Playhouse), *Gifted* (Pleasance Theatre) and *Circa* (Theater De Meervaart, The Vaults and Old Red Lion). Jenna also is Co-Executive Director of Wildcard Theatre Company.

Georgia Green (Director)

Georgia Green is an award-nominated director and writer. As director her work includes *Invisible* (Bush Theatre), *Pilgrims* (Guildhall School of Music and Drama); *Three Sisters* (LAMDA); *Human Animals* (Royal Welsh College of Music and Drama); *Twelfth Night* (ALRA); *Parliament Square* (Rose Bruford); *Outside: Three new plays by Kalungi Ssebandeke, Sonali Bhattacharyya and Zoe Cooper* (Orange Tree Theatre); *Blue Stockings* (LAMDA); *You Got Older* (LAMDA) and *The Mikvah Project* (Orange Tree Theatre, nominated for a Stage Award). Work for audio includes: *The Mikvah Project* (BBC Radio 4) and *The Get* (BBC Radio 3, October 2022). As assistant/associate director her credits include *Emilia* (LAMDA); *Dirty Crusty* (Yard Theatre); *Amsterdam* (ATC/Orange Tree Theatre, Theatre Royal Plymouth); *Out of Water* and *The Double Dealer* (Orange Tree Theatre); *Zog* (Rose Theatre Kingston/Freckle Productions/Kneehigh) and *Tiddler* (Freckle Productions). She is a lead facilitator at Cardboard Citizens, a mentor on the MFA Playwriting at Central School of Speech and Drama and has been a reader for the

Bruntwood Prize and Orange Tree Theatre. Georgia is currently one of six writers in the Emerging Writers Group at the Bush Theatre, was recently long-listed for the Verity Bargate Award in the top 20 from over 2,000 scripts, was part of the Royal Court Writers 2018–19 and was chosen from over 2,000 submissions to feature with four other writers in Pint Sized.

Joey Dawson (Producer)

Joey Dawson is the producer and owner of Reid Productions. He is currently working for the National Theatre as a digital producer. Prior to this engagement, Joey was the CEO of Wildcard Theatre Company from 2015 to 2021. Joey received his producer training from NFTS, ITC and Stage One – it was from this final organisation that he received the Stage One Bursary Award. Producing credits for theatre: *Ruckus* (2022), *Manic Street Creature* (2022), *Electrolyte* (2019), *17* (2019), *The Cat's Mother* (2018), *After Party* (2017), *A Midsummer Night's Dream* (2016). Producing credits for film: *Brother Leo's Naked* (2021), *Broken Gargoyles* (2021), *Hunch* (2020), *The Skin She Sheds* (2020).

Rachel Thomas (Associate Producer)

Rachel is an actor, producer, writer, theatre-maker and dramaturg, trained on the MA Acting course at East 15 Acting School. She is Joint Artistic Director and producer of Seventh Sense Theatre, and is an alumni of the China Plate Theatre's 2021–22 'Optimists' Producer training scheme. Producing credits include *Dog Hair* (R&D), *Memory Soldier* (Camden People's Theatre) and *Class Acts* (Golden Goose Theatre) for Seventh Sense Theatre, *Snail* (R&D, NDT), *Whole* (Arcola Theatre, Cambridge Junction, Mercury Theatre), *The Welsh Lxdies* (The Other Room Theatre), and working as assistant producer and marketing assistant for Rough Stock Theatre and Maverick Theatre. Credits as an actor include *Far Away* (Donmar Warehouse) and *The Essex Serpent* (Apple TV).

Tingying Dong (Sound Designer)

Ting grew up in Beijing and studied in the Netherlands before moving to the UK. She trained at LAMDA and is a sound designer, composer and theatre maker. Recent productions include: *The Crucible* (National Theatre); *Scissors* (Sheffield Theatres); *After The End, The Sun, the Moon, and the Stars* (Theatre Royal Stratford East); *The Breach*, *Peggy For You*, *Folk* (Hampstead Theatre); *Kathy and Stella Solve a Murder* (Roundabout/Francesca Moody Productions); *Tsunagu/Connect* (New Earth Theatre/Shoreditch Town Hall); *A Christmas Carol* (Composer, Nottingham Playhouse/ Alexandra Palace); *Two Billion Beats* (Orange Tree Theatre); *Antigone* (Storyhouse); *Klippies* (Young Vic); *My Son's A Queer (But What Can You Do)* (Turbine Theatre/Underbelly; WhatsOnStage Award for Best Off West End Production); *Jerker* (King's Head Theatre); *Ruckus* (Summerhall/Wild Card); *Imaginarium* (Online World Tour). Radio composition includes *Humane*. Short film composition includes *Medea/ Worn*; *My Last Duchess*. Nominations include Off West End Award for Best Sound Design (*The Sun, the Moon and the Stars*; *Jerker*).

Christina Fulcher (Movement Director)

Christina Fulcher is a movement director, teacher and researcher working nationally and internationally across theatre, opera, and new writing. She trained at the Royal Central School of Speech & Drama in the MFA in Movement Directing & Teaching. Christina teaches actor movement and dance at conservatoires and universities including Leeds Conservatoire, The BRIT School, LAMDA, and Mountview. She is currently training in intimacy practice, under mentorship with Ita O'Brien of Intimacy on Set. Movement and Intimacy Director credits: *The Girl on the*

Train, *Cinderella* (Barn Theatre); *Silla* (Northern Opera Group); *Dennis of Penge* (Guildhall); *The False Servant* (Orange Tree Theatre); *Cherry Jezebel* (Everyman Theatre Liverpool); *Beg for Me* (Edinburgh Fringe); *Death and Dancing* (Kings Head Theatre); *When We Died* (Edinburgh Fringe/VAULT Festival). As Movement Director: *Paper & Tin* (English Touring Opera); *Straight White Men* (Southwark Playhouse); *OUTSIDE: three new plays by Kalungi Ssebandeke, Sonali Bhattacharyya and Zoe Cooper* (Orange Tree Theatre); *Blue Stockings* (LAMDA); *STAGES, Don't Talk to Strangers* (VAULT Festival); *Into the Woods, Company, Charlie Peace* (RCCSD); *Cunning Little Vixen, Opera Scenes* (Royal Academy Opera); *The Rape of Lucretia* (Trinity Laban Conservatoire). Assistant Movement Director/Choreographer credits: *Bonnie & Clyde* (London College of Music); *Emilia* (West End; Olivier-nominated for Best Comedy); *Our House is Your Home* (Royal Opera House: Open Up Festival); *Beyond the Deepening Shadow* (Tower of London); *The Rake's Progress* (British Youth Opera); *Wasted* (Southwark Playhouse). https://linktr.ee/fulchermovement | @FulcherMovement

Simeon Miller (Lighting and Projection Designer)

Simeon has worked as a lighting designer since he graduated from Mountview Academy in 2010. He works across theatre, dance, musicals, 'gig theatre' and devised work. He enjoys contributing to new writing, especially socially and politically conscious work which amplifies oppressed and radical voices. Selected recent credits include: *Project Dictator* (New Diorama Theatre), *An Adventure* (Bolton Octagon), *Metamorphoses* (Shakespeare's Globe), *The Mob Reformers* (Lyric Hammersmith), *Subject Mater* (Edinburgh Fringe), *Black Holes* (international tour) and *High Rise eState of Mind* (UK Tour). His full portfolio and credits can be found online at www.simeon.lighting.

Jida Akil (Set and Costume Designer)

Jida Akil is a Syrian/Lebanese set and costume designer based in London. She graduated from Central Saint Martins and has since worked with notable theatres including the Young Vic as the Jerwood Assistant Designer as well as designed for acclaimed companies such as Complicité. Her designs have also been selected for exhibitions with the Prague Quadrennial and World Stage Design. Recent credits include: *Give Me The Sun* (Blue Elephant Theatre), *Funeral Flowers* (UK Tour), *Heavy Weather* (Fourth Monkey Training Company), *The 4th Country* (Park Theatre), *Darling* (The Hope Theatre), *Complicité do A-Level Drama* (UK Schools Tour), *Haramacy* (The Albany Deptford), *Solus, Just Another Soup Can, Out!* (Platform Theatre). Recent assistant/associate credits include: *Middle* (National Theatre), *The Collaboration*, *Hamlet* (Young Vic), *L'Orfeo* (Weiner Staatsoper), *My Son's A Queer (But What Can You Do?)* (Turbine Theatre).

Reuben Cohen (Video Designer)

Video design work includes: *Jews. In Their Own Words.* (Royal Court Theatre); *Into The Light* (Love Light Festival Norwich); *Creatures Of The Light* (Lumen Lite Festival Crewe); animated introductions for Tahj Miles' series *The Table Read*; *The Wider Sun* (Sam Gale and Capital Orchestra). Camera work: *Consent, Pomona, The Seagull, Red Velvet, As You Like It, Spring Awakening, The Gift* (RADA). Other professional credits: as stage musician, Taylor Mac's *A 24 Decade History of Popular Music* (Barbican Theatre).

Charlotte Ranson (Production Manager)

Charlotte studied at the University of Leeds (Theatre Production) and currently works at the Donmar Warehouse. Her credits include: as production manager, *Silence* (Donmar Warehouse), *Everyday* (New Diorama Theatre), *Manic Street Creature* (Roundabout). As deputy production manager, *Love and Other Acts of Violence* (Donmar Warehouse), *Book of Dust* (Bridge Theatre), *The Lion, The Witch and The Wardrobe* (UK Tour), *Animal Farm* (UK Tour).

Lois Simme (Stage Manager)

Lois trained at Guildhall School of Music and Drama, specialising in stage management. Credits include: *Old Bridge* (Bush Theatre), *The Game of Love and Chance* (Arcola), *The Prince* (Southwark Playhouse), *Clybourne Park* (The Park).

Naomi Shanson (Stage Manager)

Naomi Shanson is a current third year at the Royal Welsh College of Music and Drama studying stage management and technical theatre. Naomi has stage managed a multitude of productions both at university as well as in California. Her most recent credits in stage management include *Queen Margaret* (RWCMD), *Human Animals* (RWCMD), *Anna Karenina* (RWCMD), *NEW21: The Toll* (RWCMD), and *The Aliens* (Upstage Theatre).

Becky Thornton (Stage Manager)

Since graduating from the Guildhall School of Music and Drama, Becky has worked in theatre, opera, events and TV since 2018. Becky has worked at the Royal Opera House, Southwark Playhouse and Opera Holland Park. During the pandemic, Becky worked with children and adults with additional needs.

Wildcard (Producers)

Wildcard is a multi-award-winning theatre company and registered charity that revitalises theatre to engage new audiences, and nurtures emerging artists from diverse backgrounds so that they can achieve their full potential. Wildcard's work champions the 'live event' where audiences and performers meet to share stories. Accessibility is at the heart of what they do – they believe everyone should have access to high-quality theatre, interactive workshops and theatrical education.

Since its founding in 2015, Wildcard has produced multiple productions, won six awards, and toured nationally and internationally. As a registered charity, Wildcard has a big focus on providing outreach alongside its productions. Sometimes this is focused around the themes the show explores, with the aim of having a lasting impact on the communities visited. Other times, it is about strengthening the sector, such as providing workshops in schools to give young people positive role models, with the aim of increasing diversity within the industry. At the company's core is empowerment for artists, from any background, to enable them to follow their ambitions and forge their own path within this challenging industry. Part of how Wildcard do this is through associate schemes, attaching directors, producers, writers and other artists or crew to productions so that they can shadow more experienced team members. Wildcard also manages a heavily subsidised rehearsal studios, 'Wildcard Studios', in the borough of Westminster, dedicated purely to emerging artists.

Through 'Training Ground', Wildcard also runs a series of workshops facilitated by industry leaders aimed at providing training opportunities for artists to hone their craft. Additionally, Wildcard runs programmes which equip emerging companies with the tools they need to produce work on their own.

'Southwark Playhouse churn out arresting productions at a rate of knots.' **Time Out**

Southwark Playhouse is all about telling stories and inspiring the next generation of storytellers and theatre makers. It aims to facilitate the work of new and emerging theatre practitioners from early in their creative lives to the start of their professional careers.

Through our schools work we aim to introduce local people at a young age to the possibilities of great drama and the benefits of using theatre skills to facilitate learning. Each year we engage with over 5,000 school pupils through free school performances and long term in school curriculum support.

Through our participation programmes we aim to work with all members of our local community in a wide-ranging array of creative drama projects that aim to promote cohesion, build confidence and encourage a lifelong appreciation of theatre.

Our theatre programme aims to facilitate and showcase the work of some of the UK's best up-and-coming talent with a focus on reinterpreting classic plays and contemporary plays of note. Our two atmospheric theatre spaces enable us to offer theatre artists and companies the opportunity to present their first fully realised productions. Over the past 25 years we have produced and presented early productions by many aspiring theatre practitioners, many of whom are now enjoying flourishing careers.

'A brand as quirky as it is classy.' ***The Stage***

For more information about our forthcoming season and to book tickets visit **www.southwarkplayhouse.co.uk.** You can also support us online by joining our Facebook and Twitter pages.

With special thanks to:

The whole *Ruckus* team for putting your time and energy into this show. I can't thank you enough. It's been a real privilege to work with you all.

Georgia Green for your incredible directing and amazing vision. For pushing me forward with my writing and acting. And for all the chats on the secret stairs. I feel so lucky to have worked with you on this story.

Christina Fulcher and Tingying Dong for your insane talents and sticking by this show since R&D 2021. You've both made this experience wonderful.

Matthew Durkan for your incredible voice over work.

The Other Richard for the best promotional image and trailer ever.

The Wildcard founding members for believing in my idea from day one and never looking back. Every single one of you has helped me. From proofreading, R&D support, press assistance, providing feedback, moral support and encouragement. I'm so grateful to you all.

Joey Dawson for helping me to dream big and making it happen. You're brilliant.

Tom Ratcliffe for always inspiring me with your creativity and determination.

Emily Stott for sitting me down and filming the Ruckus pitch in 2019. Megan Pemberton for picking up the phone at any time to listen to the journey. My rocks.

Lizzy Connelly and Sarah Hooper for that day in room three and your consistent cheerleading. Oliver Wellington and Sam Glen for coming to read-throughs and sharing your valuable feedback.

In the early stages, Sara Joyce for those national theatre coffees. You helped to ignite a fire in my writing. Andy

Twyman, Chelsea Walker and Tommo Fowler for your dramaturg support.

Top Six for being my foundation. Andy for all your love. Mum & Dad for the endless amount of support and guidance. Lala & Keekee for always championing my work. I love you all.

Ange, Dyson, Kate, Lauren and Toni for your continuous friendship and support.

The secondary school teacher for giving me constant E's on my essays, as my writing style was too messy and complicated.

Methuen Drama for publishing my first play.

The charities and organisations for agreeing to be in the Ruckus Self Care Guide. For their continuous hard work to help victims/survivors of coercive control and domestic abuse. Working tirelessly to raise awareness of this societal issue.

Evan Stark and Jess Hill for your outstanding studies on coercive control for society.

And finally, for all the people that were willing to share their story with me. The people that work in direct services that deal with coercive control and domestic abuse daily who let me interview them. And to anyone who has shared their story of coercive control publicly with the world so we can learn, grow and change. We owe you and thank you.

*Coercive control is an act or a pattern of acts of assault,
threats, humiliation and intimidation or other abuse that
is used to harm, punish, or frighten their victim.*

Ruckus

For anyone who is, was or knows a Lou.

Characters

Lou, *twenty-eight years old*

Notes on the play

Ruckus *is a one-woman play. All the characters should be impersonated by* **Lou**. *The exception being* **Ryan**, *which is recommended to be a voice over.*

The sounds should be precise, tense and overwhelming.

The timeline is represented in the text by the following format:

– example –

The timeline has its own presence in Ruckus. *It should be explored how the timeline and* **Lou** *react together. From* **Lou** *noticing the timeline to the timeline interrupting* **Lou**. *Projection is recommended to be used to reflect the timeline as stated in the text.*

Notes on the text

Commas are not needed to be played in performance but are there for reading purposes.

Interruptions are indicated by '/'.

Quickness of change of thought indicated by '–'.

Trailing off or searching for words indicated by '. . .'.

Characters' desire to speak are indicated by also using '. . .' but alone.

Act One

Scene One

Lou *enters the space.*

She finds her place, stands still and gently smiles at everyone. She takes her time. She's preparing.

Then **Lou** *suddenly starts the rewind in the space. There's a refreshing buzz about it. Projections flashing. Various sounds.*

The space reaches its destination and stops abruptly. **Lou**'s *ready.*

Let's start from here, shall we?

I'm going to tell you everything and if you could just . . .

Watch. That'd be great.

Lou *looks to the timeline.*

– 824 days to go –

Okay.

I see him.

Lou   Hiya. Excuse me? Did your mate just pop one of our balloons?

He tells me his work colleague did. I ask him.

Lou   Why did your work colleague do that?

He's not listening to me. He's laughing with the rest of the blokes. So I'm gonna . . . I'm gonna say it a bit louder.

Lou   Oi, fucker.

He flinches. Fantastic.

Lou   I said, why did your work colleague do that?

I've stunned him. He doesn't say anything.

Lou   Tell your work colleague, I wouldn't recommend popping any more of our balloons. I'm sure he can find another way of measuring his dick.

His work colleague mutters something. Like psycho bitch. Which, wow. Really gets to me.

So I accidently pour my gin all over their shoes, and I return back to Whiny Bryony.

Bryony   Lou, if you were guarding the balloon arch like I asked you to, none of this would've happened.

Lou   Bryony, I'm sure Clintons will still be open, I can /

Bryony   You really think Clintons will have ivory white orb balloons with vine foliage?

Lou   Maybe?

Bryony   The thing is. I've worked really hard tonight. For Jess. And though it may not be your intention, I need to let you know that I feel you /

Life's quite tough for Whiny Bryony and she's always happy to share.

I catch bride-to-be Jess's eye and psychically tell her she better start her speech now. She gets it. She always does. She's the best human being on the earth.

Jess   I wanted to share with you all why I decided to propose to Charlie. And to put it simply everybody, Charlie is a sexy feminist. Take notes fellas. He let me decide when to take the relationship to the next level.

The crowd goes wild. Everybody loves Jess.

Bryony   Lou, I think it's time for the smoke machine.

Lou   I don't think it is, Bryony.

Bryony   Where's the fog fluid?

Lou   Let me just get that . . .

I head straight outside. This is why I believe I started
smoking. So I could take breaks from other humans and it to
be considered normal.

Ryan   Really sorry about what my work colleague did.

It's the guy from earlier. With two drinks. Greedy as well as a
prick. He hands out a gin and tonic with lots of ice.

Lou   I don't take drinks from strangers I'm afraid.

Ryan   Sensible. Cheers then.

He downs the whole drink. Like it's a punishment. Liquid
spilling from the sides of his mouth. Ice flops on his face. It's
satisfying.

Lou   Was that nice?

Ryan   Not really. I'm Ryan.

Lou   Pippa.

Ryan   I heard your friend call you Lou.

Lou   . . .

Ryan   Is that short for Louise?

Lou   Asking a lot of questions, Ryan.

I've not fully finished my cigarette but stubbing it out so I
can leave seems like my only option.

Ryan   Can I have your number?

Lou   No.

Ryan   Please?

Lou   Why?

He shrugs his shoulders and awkwardly smiles. Bloody hell,
he has got good teeth.

Ah shit.

Bryony   Lou, I put too much fluid in the smoke machine.
Everyone's eyes are burning. I can barely see.

Lou   Well you can see me, Bryony.

Bryony   We're literally going to need to call an ambulance.

I give this guy a fake number and head back in to open some windows. Obviously. I feel I'm the only person that has any common sense anymore.

– 823 days to go –

Jess   Charlie and I are ready to make our home, ours now, Lou.

Yeah, I'm not stupid. I knew the days of cheap rent would come to an end. Jess harks on that I'll be promoted soon. Which to be fair, I really think I will be. So it's a great chance for me to stand on my own two feet.

Jess   I'm actually really excited for you.

Jess wraps her arm around me and kisses me on the cheek. Tells me I need people like her in my life that challenge me. Of course, I don't need to move on until I find somewhere, but it would be fantastic if I could start viewings next week.

Lou *gets a text message.*

Lou   Jess. Did you give out my number last night?

Jess   I did, yes. Come on Lou, the guy seemed really nice. Plus, what's the point of having the coil if you'll never use it?

Lou *gets a text message.*

Fucking bitch Jess snatches my phone and she's replied to him. She tells me I'm welcome. That I need to put myself out there more.

– 811 days to go –

Ryan   I work as a logistical operations manager at a homeless charity.

Lou   Well fuck me, that's noble.

It's an intimidatingly nice restaurant. Ryan even orders my wine and food for me. I mock him for being a keeno and he mocks me for always talking with my hands. Touché. He wants to know more about me. I tell him there's not much to know. Hoping he won't clock the red ink on my fingers from marking my Year Four homework.

Ryan   Why do you always put yourself down?

Lou   Patriarchy.

He laughs. He gets it.

Bill's placed on the table.

Lou   Let's split. I insist.

Secretly hoped he'd pay. I'd like a free meal. Card reader. I get my card out. He pushes it back and inserts his. Cheeky. And it's done. He stands. Holds out my coat. I put my arm in the wrong hole. Twice. I'm a bit pissed. He can't stop chuckling, says how he can't keep me out of his sight for a moment, can he? Outside, I offer him a cig. He tells me it's a disgusting habit. Rude. Then he casually does up a button on my blouse.

Lou   How long does it take to get back to yours then?

Ryan   To mine?

Lou   Yeah, that's what I said.

Ryan   About twenty minutes.

Lou   Great, where is it?

Ryan   Or we can head over to the pub /

Lou   Sorry?

Ryan   To the pub? Or what do you want to do?

Lou   Well, what do you want to do?

Ryan   I don't mind.

Lou   But you don't want to go back to yours?

Ryan   Might be worth just going to the pub? Easier for you to get home then.

Lou   . . .

Ryan   Is that /

Lou   Sure let's get a drink.

Ryan   Great. You can spill a drink on my shoes again if you like?

Lou   Okay.

Ryan   I hope you don't think I'm being rude.

Lou   . . .

Ryan   I think you're great Louise. I just . . . want to be respectful to you /

Lou   So you don't want to fuck me?

Ryan   Sorry?

Lou   I'd rather know now. Not waste my time.

Ryan   Maybe we should call it a night.

Lou   Yeah, maybe you should.

Ryan   Let me get you a taxi.

Lou   Prick.

– 801 days to go –

Lou   I'm really sorry I called you a prick.

Ryan takes a polite sip from his flat white. My latte is ever so slightly burning my fingers. I'm gripping it so tightly.

Lou   I'm so sorry for last weekend.

Ryan doesn't say anything. But pulls a half smile.

Lou   My friend informed me that I acted like a dickhead.

Ryan   Is that bride-to-be Jess?

Lou   It is.

Ryan   I like bride-to-be Jess.

Lou   She thinks I'm horrendously out of practice.

So could we ignore last weekend? Start with a clean slate.

Ryan stays silent. I can't tell what he's /

Ah he grabs my latte. Walks ahead and then walks straight back.

Ryan   Hi, I'm Ryan.

He hands out my latte to me. I go to grab it.

Ryan   No, Louise. You're meant to say you don't take drinks from strangers. Let's try that again.

Lou *laughs. Then sharply stops laughing.*

There you go.

Scene Two

– 689 days to go –

Headteacher Peter tells me he wants to be completely transparent with me. He tells me all my work at Mill Hill Primary hasn't gone unnoticed. But Peter has decided to be an utter bitch and outsource for the Deputy Headship position.

Lou   That's fine, Peter. Really appreciate you taking the time to tell me face to face. Thank you.

Yes Peter, I'm okay.

– four hours later –

Lou   Of course I'm not okay, Ryan. I'm anything but okay.

Ryan sits next to me on the sofa. Hand on my knee. Softly staring at me. He's disgustingly nice.

Ryan Bub, let's talk this through.

I tell him I don't want to talk it through, and it doesn't matter as I'm an idiot and don't have nice enough clothes anyway. He doesn't get it. He's got a great career. He's set. I'm going nowhere. He tells me, I need to be kinder to myself.

Lou Ryan, can you let me be angry?

Ryan passes my phone – Jess has littered my messages – asking about the promotion – and if I've put the tenancy deposit down on the flat I saw last weekend – not that I can afford that now – no promotion – and just paid off Jess's Hen do – you know – I really thought I'd get promoted – and I chuck my phone as hard as I physically can and it slaps against the wall –

Lou Shit. Ryan, is the screen smashed?

He says it hasn't and I confirm a yes on his offer to turn my phone off.

Ryan It breaks my heart seeing you like this, Louise.

– thirty minutes later –

Ryan got me some cigs. He hates the smell, but it's a treat.

Ryan If you could, where would you move to?

Lou Maybe somewhere near the sea. Cause different.

Ryan's holding my hand. He's perfect.

Now Ryan's on his laptop. He's searching for houses in seaside towns. He's found one. We can view it at the weekend. Ryan says he can keep his job and I can easily find a teaching position. Maybe even deputy head. He's sounding crazy.

Lou Ryan, like I can afford to rent a house right now.

He tells me he'll pay more. That not everyone can be good with money. He's got a better salary. And I can blame the patriarchy for that. We'd work out money later.

Ryan Like what's actually stopping us from doing this.

I tell him I can't accept that kind of help.

Ryan But what if we're the real deal? This could be our
chance? Not copying everyone else who's trapped in their
normal lives. We're different. I feel like it's you and me
Louise. You know?

Come on, you only live once.

Lou Did you just fucking yolo me?

He smiles. Flashes those beaut teeth.

within two hours
yeah, we're doing it
we've found where we want
to move to, Newquay
yeah fucking Newquay
Ryan's got wine ah
fuck no it's champagne
bub where did you get
we drink plan kiss
order pizza with our
new joint bank account
Ryan tells me my
phone screen did smash but
we drink and eat, I
clean my teeth and floss
so we can have sex
it's two AM
running around his flat
he's doing these
funny noises and it's
we tell honest things
to each other like
I love his teeth, he's
proud of me at work,
I care too much what
other people think,

    quiet weekends,
    stuff with Ryan's parents
    it's really not nice
    to hear, it's tough but
    we're at that point when
    we can share that now
    Ryan's confused about
    my password yeah
    it's my password for
    everything okay
    jess&lou4life
    I'll change it now to
    YOLOryanlouise
    that's funny, then
    I email my notice
    to Mill Hill Primary

– 662 days to go –

Jess is going to die when she steps foot in this place. You can even see the sea from our house.

Ryan's encouraging me to let my imagination go wild, listing what else the front room needs.

Lou   Well, sofa.

I'm pacing up and down in my pyjamas. Trying to see the room from every angle.

Lou   A nice tall lamp there. Little side tables?

Ryan tells me that's a great idea.

Lou   Thank you very much darling.

    Can I put Dad's picture there?

Ryan   Of course bub.

Ryan's setting up the Wi-Fi. He's such a whiz at things like that. He set up our camera doorbell in a flash.

He asks what else?

Lou   What else? A clock? A chunky candle?

Ryan's finished with the Wi-Fi. He's looking at me.

Lou   What? Something else?

Ryan   Go nuts.

Lou   A cactus?

Ryan   Is that it?

Lou   I would say so.

Ryan   Okay. What about curtains?

Lou   Oh yeah, they're important.

Ryan   If they're that important, why did you miss them out?

And I'm . . . I'm not sure why I forgot the curtains. Our front room is facing the main street, we'll definitely need them.

Lou   Don't know, bub. Never bought curtains before.

Ryan walks out the room.

Lou   Have you bought them before?

Ryan?

Bub?

Lou *suddenly finds the duck toy.*

Scene Three

– 631 days to go –

Lou *professionally and elegantly finds farm animal toys which include a horse, cow, pig and sheep.*

– 623 days to go –

Lou   Noah, though it's really kind you want to share, Sharky can't have a bite of your Penguin bar because Sharky is a hamster. Okay?

Naughty Noah and I are in my classroom. We're making mini posters for Sharky's cage while waiting for his mum. Noah has a bit of a bad reputation. But when he's calm, he's great. Big softy.

St Oaks Primary is perfect. Fifteen-minute bus journey from where we live. Plus, you're looking at the new Deputy Head. So yeah, fuck you Mill Hill Primary.

New boss Mrs Lowe enters the classroom. Backwards.

Mrs Lowe   Oh Miss Taylor.

She looks like she's going to piss herself she's so delighted.

Lou *notices what* **Mrs Lowe** *is carrying.*

Bloody hell. It's the biggest bunch of roses I've ever seen. Embarrassingly big. Noah grabs Sharky before my desk is engulfed.

Lou   Wow, thank you Mrs Lowe.

Mrs Lowe   Oh no, it's not from me, Miss Taylor. Go on, read the card.

Lou   To Miss Taylor, a little something for your first month of work. Love R. Brackets. YOLO.

Noah's mum comes sprinting in. Noah carefully gives back Sharky and I get a quick sorry from Noah's mum. Classic kind of case you learn about in child protection training. Only she can pick him up at the moment. I mean, poor woman. She always looks exhausted.

– 589 days to go –

Giving Mum the old house tour before she needs to head home. She's touching the soil of my plants to check that they're not thirsty and realises they're moist because I'm an independent woman now. She's stroking the arm of the sofa with a massive smile on her face.

Mum   Ryan's really looking after you. Isn't he?

She's clocked the picture of Dad. Chucking me in the air as a toddler. Mum's fiddling with a tissue she's stuffed up her sleeve. Telling me I've got to keep that picture safe. It's the original photo. Like I don't already know.

Mum tells me how well organised the kitchen cupboards are. Sneaks me a twenty pound note. Tells me to get something for the house. I don't want her to leave but then Mum's Toy Boy gives me an awkward bye tap on the elbow.

Lou   Lovely to meet you.

Mum holding Ryan's shoulders, smiling and a single tear rolls down her cheek. And Ryan wipes the tear away. Does it get any better than that?

Mum tells me now that I live further away, I've got to get better at using my phone.

Lou   Mum, I'm not that bad.

Ryan catches my hand.

Ryan   Nancy, has she always spoken with her hands?

Mum confirms I always have. We're laughing. Ryan says how it drives him mad. We're all still laughing. It's a really funny day. We're waving now and they're gone. Doors locked.

Ryan pretends to collapse on the stairs with the exhaustion of the family visit. I give him a kiss. Family events are tricky for Ryan. I don't think we'll ever have his family round. So I truly mean it when I tell him how grateful I am about today, and he says how weird it was that Mum's bloke touched my waist – and I tell him it was my elbow – but Ryan's positive it was my waist and – well – my elbow is literally by my waist so it might have looked like it but it was my elbow – but he's convinced it was my waist – well – I don't know then – anyway – I go to the kitchen – no – Ryan grabs me.

Flings me over his shoulder. We're both pissing ourselves. I slide down and push him against the wall. He's tracing his fingers down my neck. He pulls a half smile.

Ryan   Already put the toothpaste on your toothbrush, bub.

Scene Four

– 551 days to go –

Cooking my classic shepherd's pie. Ryan's favourite. We have it every Wednesday.

Ryan   Finally got phase one contracts, bub.

Trying to work out when's the last time Ryan and I did something different.

Ryan   You okay Louise?

Lou   Have you ever been to Paris?

He hasn't. I tell him Jess and Charlie have just been.

Ryan   Did they like it?

Lou   Looks like they had an amazing time. Saw on Facebook they went on the Eurostar.

Ryan   Nice.

And?

Lou   Nothing. Do you know where the back door key is, bub?

Ryan   . . .

Lou   Glass is all steamed up.

Ryan finds the key. He goes to open the door.

Lou   Ryan, I can do it.

Ryan   Why has Jess's holiday bothered you so much?

Lou   It hasn't.

Ryan   Why are you talking about it then?

Lou   I'm /

Ryan   It's all you've spoken about since I've gotten in from work.

Lou   No it's fine.

Lou *notices she is talking with her hands. She stops herself.*

I tell him we should make plans for the weekend. Have fun. We've been here four months and we haven't even been to the sea yet. I don't know, I feel like at the moment all I do is work, cook and clean. Ryan's listening, nodding, staring at me.

Ryan   I . . . I don't understand why you can't be happy with what we've got.

Lou   Bub, of course I am.

Ryan   It's like you want us to compete with Jess.

Lou   That's not what /

Ryan   It's not healthy, Louise. You guys are obsessed with each /

Lou   Ryan, can you let me finish?

Ryan   . . .

Lou   All I'm saying is I'd love for us to make some plans for the weekend.

Ryan   So you have something to show off about at Jess's hen do?

I have nothing to say to that. I put the shepherd's pie in the oven and head to the front room. He follows me.

Ryan   Do I not make you happy?

Lou   Ryan, can you stop being so sensitive.

Ryan   Thanks for that Louise.

Lou   What?

Ryan   Sorry for caring. Why don't you go back on Facebook, and stalk someone else's holiday? Give Jess a call. Ask her to bring you next time. Go on. There's your phone. Do it. And don't worry Louise, I'll keep sorting the rent.

Lou   Right, Ryan. Log into our bank account now. I need to see exactly where our money /

– 527 days to go –

Jess ziplines down with her two-pound veil. Her friends erupt in screams. It's a lot.

I check in with Ryan. He asks me how it's going? I text him. I'm wearing a harness. Clipped to a tree. Fifty metres high in the air. While holding a blow-up penis. That's how it's going. I tell him I've not smoked this weekend.

Bryony   Lou?

Whines Whiny Bryony once again not understanding personal space. Ryan's typing back to me . . .

Bryony   Lou, you're not clipped in.

I'm – oh – shit I'm not – fuck – now I am – everyone's staring at me –

Bryony   You have to be clipped in at all times. Every time you move to the next obstacle.

Lou   I know.

Bryony   The red clip must never be off.

Lou   Right.

Bryony   Never. You could have died, Lou.

Lou   Well /

Bryony   No. You could've died. What a nice hen do that would be for Jess.

And she ziplines down. While holding her gaze with me. I follow and I am not surprised when no one cheers when I'm back on the ground. Jess comes over.

Jess   Lou, give me your phone. I want a picture.

Jess pulls me in close and . . .

Lou's *startled as* **Jess** *takes the photo.*

Kisses me on the lips.

Bryony   Yes girls.

Oh fuck off Whiny Bryony.

I go to grab my phone, but Jess moves away. Ignores me for a further ten seconds. She chucks my phone back to me. I look at my phone. She's been on my messages. She's . . .

Sent the picture to Ryan with a wink emoji.

Lou   Jess, why did you do that?

But she's already off with the other hens.

I text Ryan.

I can see he's online. He's seen it.

I text him again. Jess doesn't get . . .

Ryan goes offline.

– seven hours later –

I wish I could pull over and think – but I've got my live location on – so Ryan knows when to start dinner – right – Jess stole my phone – that's the truth – I'll simply explain I didn't know she would kiss me – quite forcefully actually – you know – in the picture you can see her fingers on the back of my head – I'll get the picture up to show him – no – that's a stupid idea Louise – but basically – Jess – Jess is being – Jess is being a complete bitch – Jess does what she wants because she always gets what she wants – it's not healthy – slightly obsessive really – and I'm not happy about all this – I'm really – really not –

I'm on time. You can hear the gravel move as I park up. I chew on a piece of fresh gum as I wave at the camera doorbell and head to the back door. Normally, I tell him he's being silly wanting me to use the back door for my own safety but this time it's easier if I /

Ah it's unlocked. No lights on in the kitchen.

Lou   Ryan?

I go to the living room and . . .

Tealights. Loads of tealights. Fish and chips on the table.

Ryan   Hello bub.

Lou   Bloody hell, Ryan. Nearly gave me a heart attack.

He wanted to surprise me. Thought a stodgy meal might help after the weekend I had. It's exactly what I need. Panicking over nothing. He pulls out the chair for me. Gives me a quick neck rub. Honestly, I don't know why I even . . .

– two hours later –

I find Dad's picture smashed in the bin. Photo ripped up.

We're fine now, so it's easier if I let this one . . .

Act Two

Scene One

– 498 days to go –

Lou *finds the horse, cow, pig and sheep toys. Though it's a little harder this time, she struggles to find the duck.*

She notices it's on top of the fridge. But she can't reach it.

Bullshit. I tell him it's not fair and Ryan tells me to admit I've lost.

Horse in his football boot. Cow top of hallway mirror. Pig in the make-up drawer. Sheep on the flush handle. And the duck is on top of the fridge. But I can't reach it.

We use these farm toys as a game. Ryan hides the toys around the house, and I find them when cleaning. They can be anywhere. In this case . . .

Lou It's impossible. I can't physically get it.

Ryan slides his hands to my waist. Pushes me gently against the fridge. I grab the duck. Finally.

Ryan I'll let you off this time.

– 460 days to go –

Lou Noah, can you come out from under the table please?

Otherwise, no Sharky time at the end of the day.

Noah, no need to cry. Come on. Be a big boy.

Why did you hit Gus?

I'm sorry to hear that Gus wouldn't let you sit next to him, but you can't hit people because they're doing something you don't want them to do.

What's that Noah?

Well, what kind of things do you have to do that you don't want to do?

Noah?

Noah, don't punch the table.

What kind of things?

– five hours later –

Ryan   Evenings are our time, Louise.

Lou   I know, bub.

Ryan   You're not paid enough to do meetings after work.

Lou   It won't be long. It's an urgent meeting about Noah. I'm worried /

Ryan   Have you spoken to them about your pay?

Lou   Why are you bringing up my pay, Ryan? I'm trying to tell you that I'm really worried about a student at the moment.

I've got twenty minutes. I grab the mince and veg out the fridge. I don't know what I'm gonna say to Noah's social worker /

Ryan   I don't like shepherd's pie.

Lou   It's your favourite.

Ryan   No it's not.

Lou   . . .

I'll cook something else.

I open the cupboard to /

Ryan   Cupboards really need sorting.

Lou   I know Ryan.

Ryan   Louise, you seem so stressed.

Ryan starts rubbing my shoulders. I know where this is leading to. That's why when he asks me about cleaning my teeth.

Lou   Ryan. I don't want to have sex right now.

He gives a wounded puppy look.

Lou   I have to do this meeting. Please can I use your laptop so I can access my work emails.

Do you need to watch? Or?

Thank you, bub. I won't be /

– 459 days to go –

Fuck.

Lou   Why didn't you wake me up?

Ryan said that he did shout up the stairs three times and I said I was awake – my class started fifteen minutes ago – why didn't my phone alarm go – I didn't even set one – I always do – I – fucking idiot – I'm so sweaty but shower will have to be a miss – Ryan says I need to calm down – I can't calm down – I'm going fucking crazy –

Ryan   Is that the blouse from our first date?

Lou   Yeah.

Ryan   You're going to wear that then?

Lou   Yes. What's wrong with that?

Ryan   You wore that on our first date.

Lou   Exactly. It's really old Ryan.

Ryan   Who are you trying to impress then?

Lou   What?

Ryan   When you wore that last time, you were trying to get a shag Louise.

Lou   Bloody hell Ryan.

Ryan   You always tell me to be honest.

Lou   Yeah but /

Ryan   And you're going out in an outfit that you wore to fuck me in. That's messed up, Louise.

I keep my hands glued to my thighs.

Lou   Ryan. I need to go. Can I wear this or not?

It's an old blouse, Ryan. But if you want me to change, say now. I can't be bothered with an argument when I get home.

He stands there. Staring at me. He doesn't bite. I grab my things. And a jumper. And slam the back door. I wait till I walk past the camera doorbell to get my phone out.

Lou   Jess, hi. Sorry I've missed your calls. Are you free for a quick chat?

– thirteen hours later –

Lou   This morning was unacceptable, Ryan.

I'm holding the back door key in my hand. Ryan waits on my every word.

Lou   I can't have you speaking to me like that. That's not what I want from a relationship.

Ryan   You don't deserve that. I'm so sorry, Louise.

Lou   It's not that I don't trust you. I don't trust other people.

Lou   . . .

Ryan   I'm low again if I'm honest.

Lou   You can't keep saying that then not do anything about it.

Ryan   I'll get help. Promise.

I hate myself.

Lou   Don't say that, Ryan.

Ryan   You're the best thing that has ever happened to me. You've helped me realise Louise that I've got things I have to address about myself. Everything with my parents . . . I don't know what I would do if . . .

This morning will never happen again.

Jess texts me. Asking if it's done. I delete it.

You can't only be there for the good times in relationships.

Scene Two

– 453 days to go –

Ryan   Happy one year, bub. Here's to YOLO.

– 429 days to go –

Lou   Jess, you look so beautiful.

I yank up Jess's wedding dress and she flops on the toilet. While finishing her prosecco. I give her one of my mints. I have one too. We leave the toilets, which even have their own balloon arches for fuck sake. Ryan doesn't usually drink. It's nice to see him laughing with everyone. I poke his sides and he kisses me and cups his hands around my face. He asks me if I'm having a good time. And I am.

Groom Charlie taps me on the shoulder, apologising for interrupting. I haven't seen Charlie yet tonight, so I give him the biggest hug.

Ryan   Louise, the groom doesn't want a sweaty hug on his wedding suit.

Lou   Oh yeah, sorry. Charlie, how are you feeling /

Ryan   Louise, what have you done with your hair?

Ryan flicks a moist strand of hair in my face.

Lou   Oi.

Ryan   You sure you even washed your hair today?

Lou   I washed it last night so it would hold the curl.

Ryan   You always do the weirdest styles to your hair.

Charlie tells Ryan he likes how my hair's been done.

Ryan   You do, do you?

Ryan flicks a moist strand of hair in my face. Whiny Bryony suddenly appears.

Bryony   Don't Ryan.

Ryan   What?

Ryan flicks a moist strand of hair in my face.

Bryony   That. I said don't do that, Ryan. It's rude.

Ryan cuddles me in and kisses me on the cheek.

Ryan   We find it funny, don't we?

Charlie asks if Ryan's alright.

Ryan   I'm having a great time, mate. What a wedding.

Charlie asks if Ryan's sure.

Ryan   Yup. Why don't you fucking ask again?

Lou   Let's get some water, Ryan.

Whiny Bryony has bought Jess over. Jess tells Ryan to behave.

Ryan   Alright, Mum.

Bryony calls him a dick. Jess tells him to leave.

Ryan   This is ridiculous.

The space swells and sweats.

Jess and Bryony have cocooned around me – Jess tells me that she didn't want to do this now – and Bryony asks me to blink twice if I'm not safe – what – Jess says with everything I've told her – the phone calls we've had – and now this – she's worried –

Lou   Everyone's had too much to drink, Jess. Let me speak to Ryan.

Jess tells me she loves me – she wants to help – and that I can stay with her tonight –

Ryan   Louise is not staying here with you.

Charlie and the blokes are crowding round Ryan now – he looks like a little angry kid –

Lou   Jess, Ryan's drunk. He's got a lot on right now. He doesn't /

Jess   If you say he doesn't mean it Lou, I will literally scream.

Lou   Jess, I can't leave him.

Jess tells me I can – that I need to wake the fuck up – be a strong woman about this – that I can move back in with her –

Lou   Until you kick me out again, babe?

Ryan and I are fine.

We'll go Jess. Enjoy the rest of your night.

Bryony   If you've been lying, Lou, that's really not on. It's already so hard for women to be believed.

The space overwhelms **Lou**.

Ryan   I didn't start that.

Lou   Give me the car keys Ryan.

Ryan   Can't believe Charlie was perving on you at his own wedding.

– 421 days to go –

I can't find the toy duck
anywhere, I
horse, work bag
cow, by Ryan's retainers
pig, knicker drawer and
sheep, down the toilet
and I mean I cleaned
the whole house, turned it
completely upside down
back to front and
redid the cupboards
everything is where
Ryan likes it to be
I clean again
start over, see if
I've missed something we
don't need this we've only
got back on track
he'll be home any
minute now and I
can't find the fucking
duck I always find
all of the toys and
I want to google
something like
weird spaces in a home or
good hiding places
I don't fucking know
but of course the Wi-Fi
is turned off so
Louise think, where have
you not looked yet, think
the vacuum bag, no
but I mean, where else
I take the hoover
to the garden and

shit I can't the back door
is locked, right kitchen
emptying the mess
out the vacuum bag
the dust is in my
eyes ears throat nose skin
sieving mess through my
fingers, grey thick dirt
under my fingernails
feels so gross
just to find, I can
hear the gravel move
hard door slam that means
front door's unlocking
he's here, he's here
Ryan's in kitchen
grabs an apple
other hand in pocket
I blurt out I found
the toys but the duck
I've cleaned everywhere
I can't find it, he's
listening and nodding
takes a bite from his
apple, half smiles
tells me it's not in
the vacuum bag it's –
ah
right
the
the duck was in his pocket

– 402 days to go –

I know for a fact this dentist isn't taking me seriously. I
basically had to force her to check my mouth again. She tells
me my oral care is better than average. That it's great I've
quit smoking and that I should continue to floss. So there is

no reason for there to be a bad odour present on my breath. Simply book an appointment in six months' time.

I tell her that it can't be possible. That my bad breath . . .

She asks me if I notice my bad breath? Well of course, you don't notice yourself that you have bad breath, do you?

Then she asks me who's telling me that I have bad breath. Well, my partner. She puts her clipboard down and is staring at me. She asks me, are you in a relationship where your partner is psychologically /

– four hours later –

Lou   I need a break, Ryan. I've already told Mum I'm going up. I'll call you every day I'm there.

I'm focusing on looking down the road for the bus to come. Easier looking at that than Ryan's face.

Ryan   I'll do anything if you stay.

His teeth are chattering. He didn't even bother putting on a coat when following me to the bus stop.

Lou   I'll come back on Monday evening.

Ryan   Please Louise.

Lou   I'm trying to do what's best for both of us.

Ryan   Honestly, I really can't handle this.

I can see the bus. I pull my suitcase handle up. I only have the twenty quid Mum gave me.

Lou   Sunday evening then, but Ryan /

Ryan   I can't do this.

Lou   Ryan /

Ryan   You know I don't have anyone else but you.

Lou   Ryan, please, I need to go.

The bus is pulling up.

Ryan   If you leave, that's it.

Bus doors open.

Ryan   I can't not be with you Louise. If that's the case. I don't want to be here anymore.

Lou   Ryan, don't say that.

Ryan   If you get on that bus Louise, I will hurt myself.

Lou *decides not to get on the bus.*

Lou   Give me my phone then, Ryan.

It's okay.

Hiya Mum. Yeah fine. Listen I'm so sorry but /

Scene Three

– 395 days to go –

Mrs Lowe   So sadly Noah Matthews won't be returning to St Oak. I know. His social worker emailed this morning letting us know Noah and his mum have finally entered a refuge. At least they got away. For now. Same story, isn't it? Telling a person they have a fire in their kitchen, but the person refuses to put it out. Then all you can do is slowly watch the house burn down. Then onto the next fire.

Oh and Miss Taylor, just to mention, punctuality. You've been . . . can you keep an eye on it please?

Act Three

Scene One

– 359 days to go –

Jess agrees with me that this service station is a good halfway point to meet. She hands me old post that's been delivered to hers. Really thought I changed everything to my new address.

Lou   Jess, have you had a haircut?

Jess   Not since the wedding.

I tell her it's really nice and it frames her face so well. And she . . .

She sips her tea.

Lou   How's Whiny /

Jess   Bryony's doing really great. Her balloon arch business has really kicked off.

Lou *gets a text message.*

Ryan texts me. Question about timings. Jess asks how Ryan is.

Lou   Ryan's great. He sends his love by the way. He's doing so much better Jess. We're in a really good place at the moment.

Jess smiles.

Lou   Like we have our moments. But you know, I can't see my life without him.

Jess   It's the real deal then?

Lou   Yeah.

Jess says she's really happy for me. I tell her we've landed on our feet with our guys, haven't we?

And we finish our teas.

We head to our cars. I put my live location on. I thank Jess again for the post.

Jess   Lou, I'll be driving past here next week. Shall we meet up here again?

Lou   I'm not sure.

Jess   Maybe you can leave the car here, and you can stay at mine.

Lou   Jess, I can't leave the car.

Jess   I think that would be a really good idea. Have a break. So I'll meet you here next week?

Lou   . . . Okay.

Jess   Yes?

Lou   Yeah, okay. I'll work it out. I'm sure Ryan /

Jess give me the biggest hug and . . .

Lou *holds this moment a little longer.*

Neither of us knew that would be our last hug.

Scene Two

– 340 days to go –

Sharky the hamster has nearly chewed through all of Noah's posters. But I don't want to take them down. Sharky's staying with me for half term break. As if there is anything I can do to get into Mrs Lowe's good books, I'm bloody doing it.

Ryan passes me a bowl of grapes. He tells me the cupboards look perfect, which I already know. He's trying. Letting me see Jess, having Sharky. But I'm exhausted. Knowing he could . . .

Ryan   Are you going to the half term meal tomorrow?

I tell him I don't have to go. He suggests he could drop me off and pick me up. Get some money out on the way. I deserve a nice night. Have a few drinks. He'll pick me up at nine thirty. I tell him I don't mind nine. But we agree on nine thirty. Great.

I ask Ryan if he wants to feed some grapes to Sharky. He does. Sharky loves it. Her little hands are clasping Ryan's thumb. She's so delicate.

Ryan   Didn't know hamsters had such long whiskers.

Lou   It's to compensate for their weak eyesight.

He's laughs at the fact I knew that straight away. I explain that my students have asked me every possible question there could be about hamsters. My personal favourite, why does hamsters poo look like brown tic tacs.

He laughs. He gets it.

– 339 days to go –

Mrs Lowe is completely hammered. And us staff are loving it. She's sharing unexpressed feelings.

Mrs Lowe   I want to let you all know that you lot are like family to me.

Mrs Lowe goes for a group hug and knocks over two bottles of wine. We're all in stitches. She's mortified and heads to the bar for napkins and that's when I see Ryan standing at the bar.

It's just nine. How long has he . . .

Ryan   Lovely to finally meet you, Mrs Lowe. I've heard such great things.

Mrs Lowe goes to shake Ryan's hand. But to everyone's entertainment, he picks her up and spins her round. The staff are clapping. Even other people in the restaurant cheer. He's actually doing a great job of introducing himself to everyone. Ryan finally comes to me and gives me a big kiss

which all of the staff whoops at. Someone shouts out she
can't remember the last time her husband was romantic like
that. We're all laughing. I say my goodbyes and follow Ryan,
who's already nearly halfway across the car park.

Lou   Hey?

Ryan   Stop walking so slowly Louise.

Lou   Ryan, what's /

Ryan   You're late.

Lou   No I'm not.

Ryan   Yes, you are, we said nine.

Lou   We said nine thirty.

We get in the car. Seatbelts on. Doors locked. Ryan pulls out
a piece of paper out of his pocket . . .

I knew I should've ripped that up.

Ryan   Why did you lie?

Lou   I didn't.

Ryan   You didn't tell me you received this letter, right?

I got offered a job interview for the deputy headship role. At
my old school, Mill Hill Primary. I didn't apply for it, but
they must've /

Ryan   So you lied.

It's not that I purposely didn't tell Ryan. I put the letter in
the bin straight away. I didn't want him to think /

Ryan   Are you trying to leave me?

Lou   Of course not.

Ryan   How am I going to believe anything that comes out
your mouth?

Ryan turns the car on. Sharply pulls out from the side of the road. He's driving. He's gripping the steering wheel tightly.

Lou   Ryan, I'm not trying to leave you.

Ryan   Then why did they send you this letter?

Lou   I don't know. It was sent to Jess first then /

Ryan   Of course Jess has something to do with this. She always has.

Lou   Ryan.

Ryan   Your behaviour is completely unacceptable.

Lou   Ryan, I didn't apply for   **Ryan**   Listen. Stop
the job. It's not my fault.   interrupting me. Shut up
                                                                        Louise.

Lou   Ryan, don't shout at me /

Ryan   Don't even try it, Louise. You don't get to make me look like the bad guy here.

Lou   I'm not trying to.

We're on the motorway now.

Ryan   Everything I do is for you. Do you really think someone else would be there /

Lou   I know Ryan.

Ryan   Stop interrupting me. You're making this harder on yourself.

I'm watching the little orange speed dial going up and we're overtaking every car.

Lou   Ryan, pull over. I want   **Ryan**   You don't get to lie
to get out Ryan, you're   and leave. So you don't
scaring me. Pull over.   get to fuck me over. No
Ryan?   one gets to fuck me over.

Ryan reaches to the keys in the ignition to

Lou   Ryan, what the fuck are you doing?

The space plunges into darkness.

The car it's – it's still moving – the motorway road in front of us has completely disappeared and I can't – I can't believe he actually – I try and grab the keys from his right hand and – he moves his hand away – what – he moves his hand away – Ryan give me the keys – bub – give me the — we're going to hit something – I don't think the car behind us can see us – Ryan – look in the mirror – they can't see us – I don't think he's going to put the keys back in – he's not – is he? – the car lights behind us is filling our car now – fuck this is really going to be it if – Ryan – put the keys back in – Ryan – I'm – I'm so sorry Ryan – I'm sorry – Ryan please – it's coming – Ryan I'm sorry – I'm /

– three hours later –

We're both kind of dozing on the sofa. Ryan's holding my hand. He's calm. And I'm lighter. He asks for some water. Good shout. My head's pumping. Head to the kitchen. I need to be more careful. Think before I . . .

Lou *stops dead in her tracks. Something has caught her eye.* **Lou** *goes over to have a further look.*

Sharky's not in her cage.

Lou *looks around.*

She's . . .

Lou *finds what she was looking for. She reacts from her gut /*

Scene Three

– 338 days to go –

I don't think I'll ever
meet someone who
loves me as much as

Ryan loves me and
hates me as much as
Ryan hates me, I'm
not stupid by the
way, I know this can't
it's early, I'm in
my dressing gown and
Ryan hands me a
cup of tea, he's smiley
chatty, saying
today we really
should go to the sea
still can't believe we've
not done that yet, he
takes his boxers off
looks over his shoulder
wiggles his bum
I smile, letting
the hot tea only
burn my lips, I'm not
swallowing a drop
he's going into
the shower and I
turn his bedside lamp
off while looking for
my phone because it
is my phone, it's mine
can't see it anywhere
I ask him if
he needs a shirt ironed
he does so I'm
heading downstairs the
noise of the shower
echoing around
the house I've got eight
ten minutes max
so I'm

The space reacts, beginning to slowly melt and caving in.

grabbing the
cookbook where I've kept
the twenty pound note, no
phone, car keys, where
is the back door key
cause I'm gonna go
I have to be fast
camera doorbell will
see the direction
I'll go in so I'll
run to the bus stop
train station, check times
ticket, board the train
go to Mum's, but she'll
be devastated
she loves that I'm settled
safe with Ryan
I'll go to Jess and
tell her everything
be accountable
that I've missed her so
but Ryan knows where
everybody lives
I can't put Mum and
Jess through that it's not
fair to bring them into
this mess I've made
this mess that I'm still
trying to protect
you know with my job
I'm trained to look out
for this exact
situation, stand on
a chair, checking
the tops of the cupboards
I could go to the

police and tell them
what exactly, I've lied
I've done things wrong
I'd waste their time when
they could help someone
else, police would ask
me what they should do
I wouldn't want
family contacted
I wouldn't want to
lose what I have and
wouldn't want Ryan
in trouble as he's
made a mistake
because he needs help and
if I'm not here
whose going to help him
the key was on top
of the fridge, fucker
the shower noise stops
it's now, I unlock
the back door, instant
rush of cool air and
I'm gonna go and
work it out and . . .

The space reaches highest point of intensity.

I can't.

The space finally caves in. It's destructive and boiling.

Scene Four

– 338 days to go –

The space neutralises. **Lou** *looks at the timeline. Takes in the final days to go.*

Did you see it?

It . . . it can be confusing. I can sometimes get a bit stuck in it. But did you see it? I really want you to. I don't want you . . .

I think you know what I'm going to talk about next. And if you don't, that's fine. This isn't nice, but I really think I owe it to you to tell you.

Ryan never laid a finger on me. Until three hundred and thirty-eight days from now. He grabbed my neck. Squeezed. And at that moment, everything was still. The ruckus stopped. We were back in reality. I don't think either of us could believe what was happening. And that it was happening to us. It took seven minutes. Then that was it. It's like Ryan and I slotted perfectly together. We were built for it.

I'm purposely not going into all of the details of that day. You're numbed to that information by now, surely? You hear of it all the time through percentages or one in however many women. Don't get me wrong, statistics are important. Otherwise, how do we learn? Grow. Change. How do we do that without statistics? I actually think I'm pretty selfish that I thought I'd never be one.

It's the beginning for me. The first sixteen months. How it happened. The exact points. What could I have done? Hoping to find some greater meaning to it all. Otherwise, it's such a waste, isn't it? A complete waste. A predictable waste.

Did you see it?

Lou *waits, even searches, for a response. It's an uncomfortable amount of time. Until she realizes . . .*

Again.

Lou *prepares herself to start again.*

By the way, I'm fucking furious. I'm just cautious you won't take this seriously if I get too angry.

Lou *exits the space.*

Act One

Scene One

Lou *enters the space.*

She finds her place, stands still and gently smiles at everyone. She takes her time. She's preparing.

Then **Lou** *suddenly starts the rewind in the space. There's a refreshing buzz about it. Projections flashing. Various sounds.*

The space reaches its destination and stops abruptly. **Lou***'s ready.*

Let's start from here, shall we?

I'm going to tell you everything and if you could just . . .

Watch. That'd be great.

Lou *looks to the timeline.*

– 824 days to go –

Okay.

I see him.

Lou   Hiya.

Blackout.